DATE DUE			

INVENTIONS
in science

INTO
SPACE

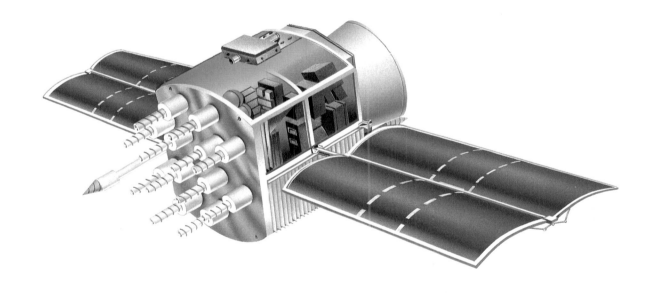

NIGEL HAWKES

GLOUCESTER PRESS
NEW YORK • CHICAGO • LONDON • TORONTO • SYDNEY

*First published in the United States
in 1993 by*
Gloucester Press
95 Madison Avenue
New York, NY 10016

Printed in Belgium

Library of Congress
Cataloging-in-Publication Data

Hawkes, Nigel
    Into space / Nigel Hawkes.
        p. cm. -- (Inventions In Science.)
    Includes index.
    Summary: Examines the scientific
technology involved in space exploration and
how it has affected our day-to-day lives.
    ISBN 0-531-17416-6
    1. Outer space--Exploration--History--
Juvenile Literature.
2. Astronautics--Social aspects--Juvenile
Literature. -[1. Outer space--Exploration--
History. 2. Astronautics--Social aspects.]
I. Title. II. Series.
TL793.H37 1992
629.4--dc20
93-13468   CIP   AC

Design:	David West
	Children's Book Design
Designer:	Stephen
	Woosnam-Savage
Editor:	Jen Green
Picture researcher:	Emma Krikler
Illustrators:	Ian Thompson,
	David Russell

The author, Nigel Hawkes, is science
correspondent of *The Times* newspaper in
London, and has written many science books
for children.

The consultant, Steve Parker, is a writer and
editor in the life sciences, health, and medicine.

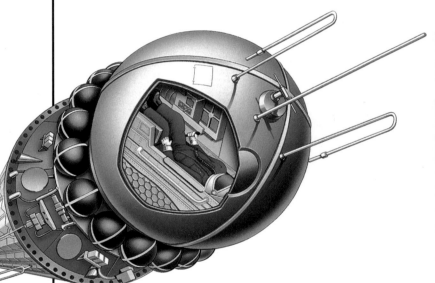

PHOTOCREDITS
*Abbreviations: T-top, M-middle, B-bottom, L-left,
R-right*

*Front cover top & pages 4 T, 24 T, 25 BR, 26 B, 27
BR, 28 & 29 TL: Frank Spooner Pictures; front
cover bottom & pages 10, 15 L, 21 M, 27 TL & 30
B both: Novosti RIA; 4B, 5 both, 6-7, 8, 9 T both,
12 both, 13 BR, 16, 17 all, 18, 20 both, 21 T, 22
both, 24 B, 25 BL, 27 BL & 30 B: NASA; 6 T &
29 B both: David Hardy, Astro Art; 6 B, 9 B, 14, 30
T & 31 T: Hulton Deutsch; 7 T & 11 B:
Popperfoto; 7 B & 29 T both; Mary Evans Picture
Library; 11 T & M, 13 T, 19 M, 25 T, 26 T & 27
TR: Science Photo Library; 13 BL: Spectrum
Colour Library; 15 R & 19 B: Roger Vlitos; 19 T
& 23: Hutchison Library.*

CONTENTS

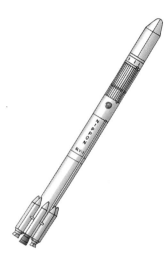

SPACE TODAY	4
DREAMS OF SPACE TRAVEL	6
THE SPACE AGE BEGINS	8
THREE, TWO, ONE, LIFT-OFF!	10
MAN ON THE MOON	12
LAUNCH VEHICLES	14
THE REUSABLE SPACECRAFT	16
ROCKETS FOR RENT	18
LIVING IN SPACE	20
SATELLITE REVOLUTION	22
SPIES IN THE SKY	24
SECRETS OF THE UNIVERSE	26
THE FUTURE OF SPACE TRAVEL	28
CHRONOLOGY	30
GLOSSARY	31
INDEX	32

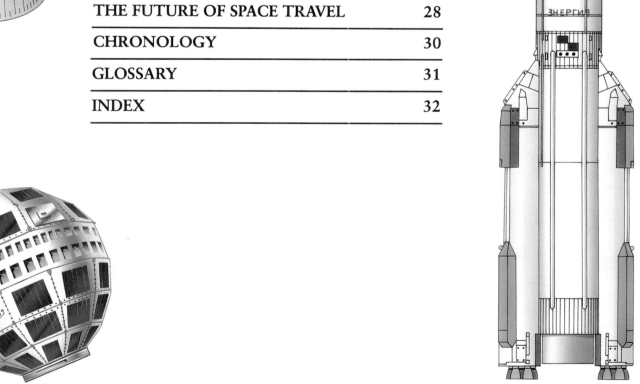

SPACE TODAY

Since the Space Age began in 1957, space has become a huge industry driven by pride, prestige, and hope of profit. Men have stood on the Moon, while satellites and space probes have explored distant planets. On Earth, space science has changed daily life. Communications satellites bring TV pictures and inexpensive telephone calls from around the world. Manufacturers use technology and materials developed for spacecraft. But would all this have happened without the Cold War, and will it continue now there is increasing harmony? This book looks at what space exploration has achieved and the impact it has had and will have on our daily lives.

The final frontier
Space enthusiasts say that space travel is our last great challenge. It may one day reveal incredible knowledge. Opponents say it wastes billions of dollars that could be used to relieve hardship in the world and uses vital resources.

Buran

Maneuvering rockets

Space junk
After thirty years of launches, dead satellites, jettisoned hatches, old booster rockets, and miscellaneous junk now orbit the Earth in a thickening cloud. In the popular orbits used by communications satellites, space now has to be rationed out by international agreement.

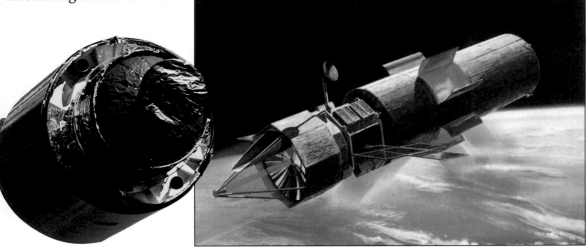

Dangers
Space flight may endanger the lives of ordinary people. Satellites have crashed to Earth in large pieces. Their radioactive cargoes can spill over the land. Some, like this anti-missile satellite (left) may carry laser weapons.

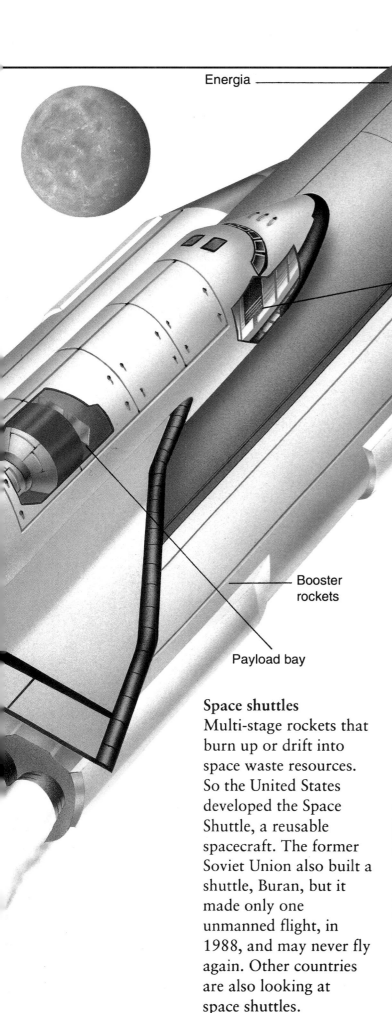

Energia

Flight computers

◀Unlike the U.S. shuttle, Buran has no rockets but rides piggyback on the powerful Energia booster to get into orbit.

Booster rockets

Payload bay

Medical advances
Monitoring the health of astronauts in space helps doctors understand how the human body works. In space, you grow one to two inches taller and your wrinkles disappear, thanks to weightlessness. With no exercise, your muscles and bones weaken. These changes are not permanent.

Space shuttles
Multi-stage rockets that burn up or drift into space waste resources. So the United States developed the Space Shuttle, a reusable spacecraft. The former Soviet Union also built a shuttle, Buran, but it made only one unmanned flight, in 1988, and may never fly again. Other countries are also looking at space shuttles.

The space industry
The space business provides a living for thousands of designers, technicians, craftspeople, and computer experts. These jobs may extend into space itself. Without gravity, it may be possible to make better products than on Earth. Crystals grow better, and some drugs are easier to manufacture.

DREAMS OF SPACE TRAVEL

The first rockets were made in China in the 13th century. From the beginning, rockets were used as weapons of war, to carry explosives and target an enemy. By 1806, rockets were being used against Napoleon's fleet, but they were inaccurate. In the early 20th century two men dreamed of using rockets to travel into space: Konstantin Tsiolkovsky, a Russian, and Robert Goddard, an American. Independently they realized that only the rocket, which carried all its own fuel with it, could escape the pull of Earth's gravity, and travel across the vast emptiness of space.

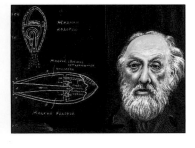

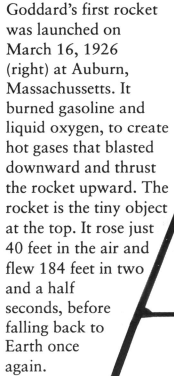

Tsiolkovsky's idea
Konstantin Tsiolkovsky, a schoolteacher, worked out the basic principles of space flight around 1903. He realized that to escape the Earth's gravity, several powerful rockets would be needed. These rockets could be arranged in stages, each stage taking over as the other ran out of fuel.

Goddard
Robert Goddard, an American physicist, was the first to design a proper high-altitude rocket. After people laughed at his early efforts, he worked more secretly at his launch pad in Roswell, New Mexico.

German interest
In the early 1930s, the German Army became interested in developing rocket-powered missiles. An early result of their experiments was the VFR rocket (below).

Goddard's first rocket was launched on March 16, 1926 (right) at Auburn, Massachussetts. It burned gasoline and liquid oxygen, to create hot gases that blasted downward and thrust the rocket upward. The rocket is the tiny object at the top. It rose just 40 feet in the air and flew 184 feet in two and a half seconds, before falling back to Earth once again.

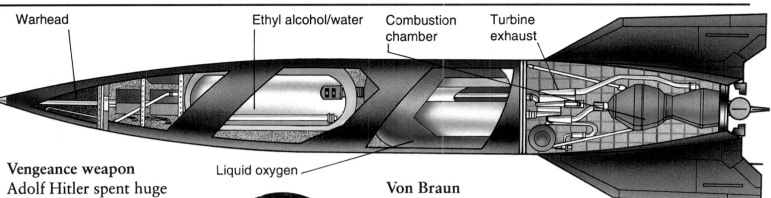

Warhead

Ethyl alcohol/water

Combustion chamber

Turbine exhaust

Liquid oxygen

Vengeance weapon
Adolf Hitler spent huge German resources on rockets. In 1942 the prototype A-4 rocket reached a height of 150 miles from the launch pad at Peenemunde on the Baltic Sea. An A-4 later became the first man-made object to leave the Earth's atmosphere. It was also known as the V-2, the V for Vergeltungswaffe, or vengeance weapon.

Von Braun
Wernher von Braun (left) became leader of the German rocket team designing missiles. During World War II 1,403 V-2s were fired at London, killing 2,754 people. After the war, von Braun went to the United States, became an American citizen, and helped build the first American rockets.

The V-2 in action
The V-2 used a steam turbine to pump alcohol and liquid oxygen from separate tanks into the rocket motor. Here the gases mixed and fired in a continuous explosion that blasted the rocket forward. But the V-2 was not very accurate.

Space fiction
The inspiration for Von Braun and many others came from writers like Jules Verne. Verne wrote a story about a voyage to the Moon as early as 1865, anticipating many of the features of the Apollo Moon landings 100 years later. H.G. Wells, in "War of the Worlds" portrayed an invasion of Earth by intelligent but unfriendly creatures from Mars.

THE SPACE AGE BEGINS

World War II ended in 1945, but the Cold War, an era of confrontation between the United States and the Soviet Union, began soon after. Both countries developed rockets to display their military might and national pride. Under a brilliant leader, Sergei Korolyev, the Soviets had by 1956 built a giant rocket, the SS-6, capable of carrying a two-ton bomb 4,000 miles. To demonstrate the rocket, Korolyev was ordered to launch a satellite, a small object that would stay in space, and circle around the Earth. On October 4 1957, the satellite Sputnik 1 was launched. The Space Age had begun.

Launchers

Sputnik's SS-6 launcher was big and simple, but very effective. It consisted of a central core, with four strap-on boosters to increase lift off power.

Compared to the Soviet design, the American rockets (below) were lighter and more delicate in construction. They used high-technology fuel tanks instead of the thick-walled steel tanks of the SS-6. Less power meant that American satellites had to be light. This gave a boost to the development of min-iaturized electronic devices such as new transistors, which were soon used in portable radios and other everyday objects.

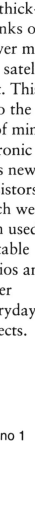

A-1
Sputnik

Vanguard

Juno 1

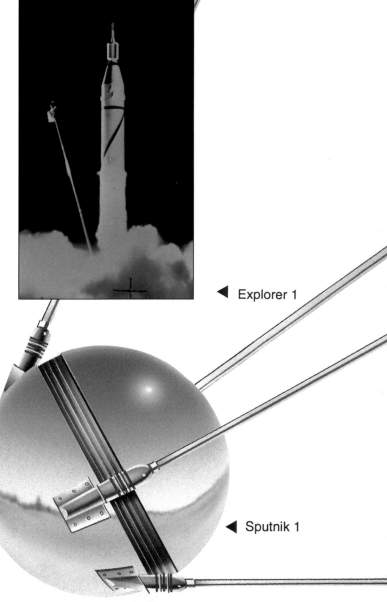

◀ Explorer 1

◀ Sputnik 1

The response to Sputnik

By late 1957, the United States was ready to match Sputnik with a satellite of its own. But the first launch, of a Vanguard rocket with a tiny 3.4 pound satellite, was a dismal failure. It rose only a few feet before crashing back to the launch pad and exploding in a ball of flame. In desperation, the United States turned to Wernher von Braun, whose satellite project had been in need of money.

American success

Von Braun put together a Jupiter C rocket and a satellite called Explorer. This was launched successfully on January 31, 1958 (see the photo on the opposite page). Explorer 1 was a much smaller satellite than either of the first two Sputniks which preceded it into space. Other early American launches met with less success: a Mercury rocket suffered premature engine cut-off during its launch in 1960 (above left).

In April 1958, the National Aeronautics and Space Administration (NASA) was created, to survey the Moon and put a man into space. It has been a force in world science and politics ever since.

▲ NASA's first office building in Washington D.C.

Sputnik

Sputnik 1 (left) was a simple metal sphere that weighed 184 pounds. Its transmitter emitted a series of beeps. In November 1957, the much larger Sputnik 2 carried a passenger: the dog Laika, who became the first space traveler.

Voices from the sky

A satellite is an object that goes around another. Scientists realized that artificial radio satellites could relay radio, TV, and telephone signals around the Earth. The first was Telstar, (below right) launched by the U.S. in 1962. In 1965, Early Bird became the first geostationary satellite. People could watch the Beatles (below) live on TV beamed from another continent.

The van Allen belts

One of the instruments on Explorer 1 was designed to count and measure electrically charged particles in space. This instrument led to the first space discovery. James van Allen, the scientist responsible, noticed that at certain heights the counter seemed to stop working, and he realized it had been overloaded. The reason was a region in space dense with charged particles - now known as the van Allen belts. These sometimes disrupt radio communications.

THREE, TWO, ONE, LIFT-OFF!

Early in 1959, the Soviet Union began building a spacecraft to carry a man into orbit. Vostok ("East") was designed to be virtually automatic in operation, so that unmanned launches to test its systems could be carried out first. After two successful test launches, Yuri Gagarin was shot into space on April 12, 1961, made a single orbit of the Earth and ejected at a height of 23,000 feet before parachuting down. A human being had entered space for the first time, an event as historic as the voyage of Christopher Columbus.

Mercury and Gemini

In 1961, the United States succeeded in putting men in space. John Glenn achieved a complete orbital flight the next year. These early flights were in one-person Mercury space-craft. After the United States declared its intention of making a manned Moon landing, two-man Gemini spacecraft were used to develop skills like docking, needed for the lunar mission.

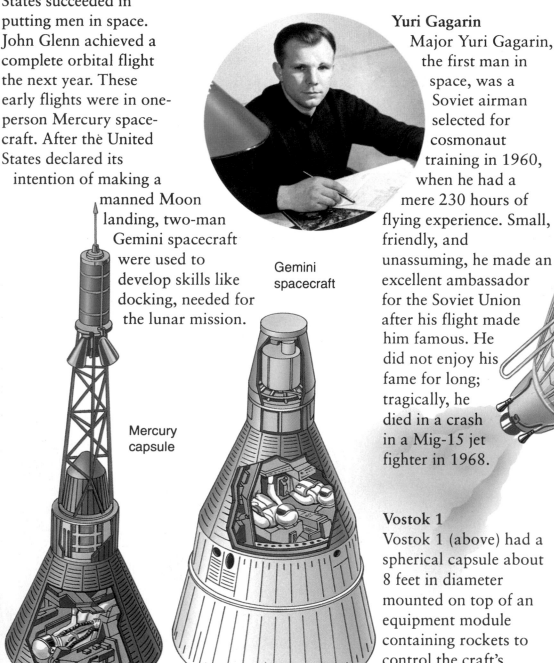

Mercury capsule

Gemini spacecraft

Yuri Gagarin

Major Yuri Gagarin, the first man in space, was a Soviet airman selected for cosmonaut training in 1960, when he had a mere 230 hours of flying experience. Small, friendly, and unassuming, he made an excellent ambassador for the Soviet Union after his flight made him famous. He did not enjoy his fame for long; tragically, he died in a crash in a Mig-15 jet fighter in 1968.

Vostok 1

Vostok 1 (above) had a spherical capsule about 8 feet in diameter mounted on top of an equipment module containing rockets to control the craft's position and to slow it down for reentry. At the time the Soviet Union declared that Gagarin had stayed in his capsule until landing, to give the impression that their space program was more advanced.

Cost of manned flight
Each manned launch costs hundreds of millions of dollars. Astronauts' vehicles are large, heavy, and fitted with life support systems. They need still more powerful launchers and more preparation.

▶ The Vostok capsule preserved in the Moscow space museum

◀ Vostock 1 carried Yuri Gagarin into orbit

▼ Painting of the launch of Vostock 1

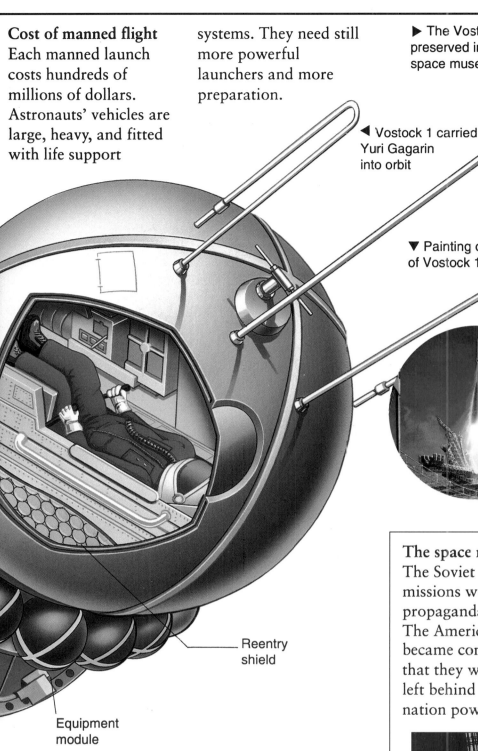

Reentry shield

Equipment module

Soviet successes
In 1964, the USSR put three men into orbit in Voshkod 1. On Voshkod 2 in 1965, Alexsei Leonov made the first space walk, then struggled to get back into the spacecraft. After landing 1800 miles off course, the crew spent a night hiding from wolves before rescue.

The space race
The Soviet manned missions were a huge propaganda success. The American people became concerned that they were being left behind by the only nation powerful enough to threaten them with war. The government voted money for space programs, and 5,000 people jammed Central Park to watch John Glenn become the first U.S. astronaut.

Kennedy's promise
President John F. Kennedy, looking for a popular crusade to mark his presidency, asked for the Moon. On May 25, 1961 he promised that the United States would land a man on the Moon, and return him safely to Earth, before the decade was out. These were bold words, for America had not yet succeeded in putting a man into orbit.

MAN ON THE MOON

NASA's Apollo Moon-landing program was a triumph of organization and technology. It required a new rocket, a new spacecraft, and a new plan for landing on the Moon and then departing safely. The rocket was the three-stage Saturn V, designed by Wernher von Braun. The spacecraft was Apollo, which could divide into two while in Moon orbit, leaving the command module aloft while two explorers descended to the surface in the lunar module. In July 1969, it all worked flawlessly. Kennedy's promise was kept, and men set foot on the Moon for the first time.

Rehearsals

A series of missions tested every aspect of the Apollo design. The first flights, Apollo 5 and 6, were unmanned; Apollo 7 took men into Earth orbit, Apollo 8 into lunar orbit. Apollos 9 (right) and 10 tested the lunar module, first around the Earth and then in lunar orbit. Finally all was set for the first landing by Apollo 11. There were five more Moon landings.

Setbacks

Though mainly successful, the Apollo program had its failures. In 1967, a fire in Apollo 12 (above) on the launch pad killed three astronauts. In 1970 an explosion on Apollo 13, two days after launch meant the Moon landing was canceled, and the astronauts only just managed to return safely to Earth.

Lunar takeoff

One key to the success of the Apollo mission was a reliable rocket to lift the lunar module from the surface of the Moon. Without it, the astronauts would have been trapped. When the first design proved troublesome, a new one was created.

▼ Rocket power
The Saturn V rockets when launched created the loudest sound man has ever produced – 190 decibels. Their five first-stage engines burned 15 tons of fuel a second.

Five J-2 engines

Five F-1 engines

First stage

Landing conditions

The nature of the Moon's surface was something which concerned American scientists. Some thought it consisted of a layer of dust 30 feet thick that would swallow Apollo. Unmanned flights by Surveyor spacecraft proved this was not the case, and sent back pictures of the surface.

Lunar experiments

On the Moon, Armstrong and Aldrin set up a laser reflector to enable scientists to measure the distance to the Moon to within 6 inches. They also set up instruments to study "moonquakes," and collected rocks to bring back to Earth.

Launch escape system

Command module

Service module

Lunar module

Third stage

J-2 engine

Second stage

Studying the Moon

The astronauts traveled in an electrically-powered Lunar Rover to examine the landscape. Six Apollo landings found that the Moon was a dead planet 4.6 billion years old, with a deeply cratered surface and rolling hills.

One giant leap

"One small step for man, one giant leap for mankind," said Neil Armstrong as he set foot on the Moon on July 21, 1969. Millions watched on live TV back on Earth. Alongside him was Buzz Aldrin, while Michael Collins waited in the orbiting command module.

Neil Armstrong

Neil Armstrong was a test pilot who had served in the Korean War. A cool, careful flyer, his skill helped Apollo land safely when he changed course at the last minute to avoid rough ground.

Link-up

In 1975, NASA agreed to a joint space mission with the Soviet Union, in which an Apollo and a Soyuz spacecraft would link in orbit. This "handshake in space" was to begin a new era of cooperation. The mission went well, and U.S. and Soviet astronauts shared a meal (below).

LAUNCH VEHICLES

Throw a ball in the air and it will come down, pulled by the force of gravity. Throw it hard enough and it will never come down, because it has enough speed to escape Earth's gravity and fly into space. This is the job of a rocket-powered launch vehicle. In theory, one giant rocket could reach space, but it would be carrying unnecessary weight as it reached the edge of space. In a multi-stage rocket, each stage falls away as it runs out of fuel, leaving a lighter rocket to fly higher.

Into orbit
Three rocket stages are enough to reach space (below). Strap-on boosters may be used as part of the first stage. They provide extra power during the first part of the flight, when gravity is strongest. When they burn out they are jettisoned and fall into the sea. The second and then the third stages of the rocket burn to bring the cargo or payload – in this case, satellites – to orbiting height.

Early rockets
The first American manned launches were made by Redstone rockets, a development of the V-2. For the orbital flights the more powerful Atlas rocket was used.

Launch vehicles
Only the United States and the Soviet Union have developed rockets powerful enough for manned missions. The biggest is the Soviet Energia (below right and inset opposite) which can lift 100 tons into Earth orbit. Other nations have built smaller rockets for launching satellites, including Ariane 4 (center) produced for the European Space Agency (ESA). Japan has a satellite launcher (left) and is planning a manned space program.

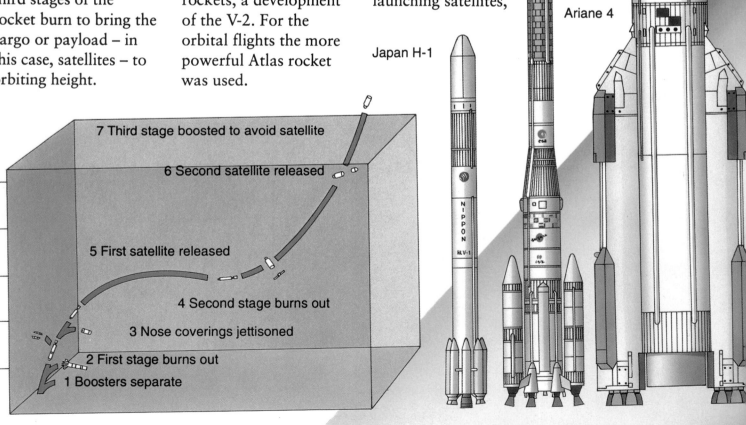

7 Third stage boosted to avoid satellite

6 Second satellite released

5 First satellite released

4 Second stage burns out

3 Nose coverings jettisoned

2 First stage burns out

1 Boosters separate

Japan H-1

Ariane 4

Energia

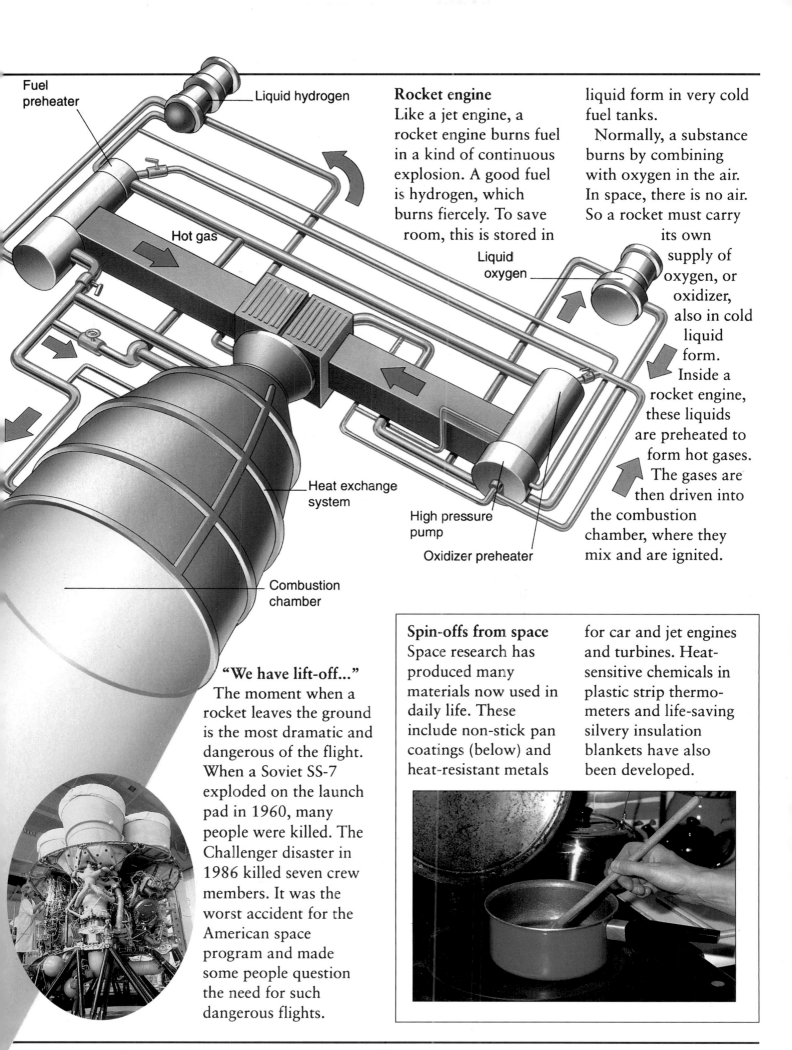

Fuel preheater

Liquid hydrogen

Hot gas

Liquid oxygen

Heat exchange system

High pressure pump

Oxidizer preheater

Combustion chamber

Rocket engine

Like a jet engine, a rocket engine burns fuel in a kind of continuous explosion. A good fuel is hydrogen, which burns fiercely. To save room, this is stored in liquid form in very cold fuel tanks.

Normally, a substance burns by combining with oxygen in the air. In space, there is no air. So a rocket must carry its own supply of oxygen, or oxidizer, also in cold liquid form. Inside a rocket engine, these liquids are preheated to form hot gases. The gases are then driven into the combustion chamber, where they mix and are ignited.

"We have lift-off..."

The moment when a rocket leaves the ground is the most dramatic and dangerous of the flight. When a Soviet SS-7 exploded on the launch pad in 1960, many people were killed. The Challenger disaster in 1986 killed seven crew members. It was the worst accident for the American space program and made some people question the need for such dangerous flights.

Spin-offs from space

Space research has produced many materials now used in daily life. These include non-stick pan coatings (below) and heat-resistant metals for car and jet engines and turbines. Heat-sensitive chemicals in plastic strip thermo-meters and life-saving silvery insulation blankets have also been developed.

THE REUSABLE SPACECRAFT

Conventional rockets are used just once, then thrown away. The space shuttle is different; it takes off vertically, like a rocket, enters space as a spacecraft, and then returns and lands on a runway like an aircraft. The idea was to make spaceflight simpler and cheaper, but the results have been disappointing. To put a satellite into orbit with NASA's space shuttle costs up to $250 million, no less than a conventional rocket. The popular dream of ordinary people paying for a space ride is still many years away.

Development

The design of the shuttle drew on experience from a series of rocket planes developed in the United States. The first of these, the Bell X-1, launched in mid-air from beneath a B29 bomber, was the first aircraft to exceed the speed of sound in 1947. Later models (below) showed the rounded shape and V-shaped delta wings of the shuttle, designed to resist the intense heat of reentry and then to glide swiftly to a landing.

X-15

The Bell X-15 rocket plane (above), tested in the 1960s, reached speeds of more than 4,000 mph and attained heights of 67 miles, the very edge of space.

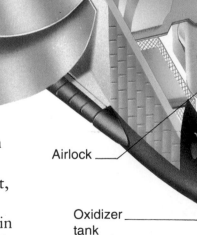

Satellite payload

Fuel tanks

Payload handling controls

Airlock

Oxidizer tank

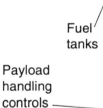

X 24A

M2F3

X 24B

The shuttle

The shuttle is built of aluminium alloy, covered with ceramic tiles to protect it from the heat of reentry. The cargo bay is 60 feet long by 15 feet wide, which is about the size of a railway freight wagon. The doors are made of carbon-fiber reinforced plastic. The stubby wings allow the shuttle to glide, though very fast, and land at more than 200 mph The flight deck is the upper level at the front, with the galley and sleeping berths below in the mid deck area. Each shuttle costs about $1.1 billion.

First flight

The space shuttle Columbia lifted off for its maiden flight in 1981. In general, the shuttle program has been successful. It launches satellites regularly, carries out experiments in space, and also does secret military work. It has made dramatic rescues.

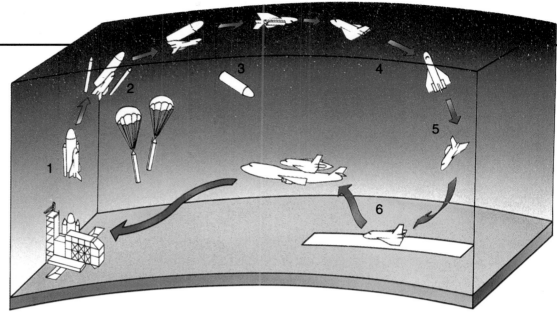

Flight plan

The flight sequence of the shuttle appears above. For lift-off (1), the shuttle uses its three main engines, plus two boosters. Extra fuel is carried in a huge internal tank. After two minutes, the boosters burn out and parachute into the sea (2). Six minutes later, the main engines stop, and the fuel tank is released (3). The final step into space is made by smaller orbital engines (4). After landing (5), a Boeing 747 returns the shuttle to the launch pad (6).

International rescue

In 1992 (below) three shuttle astronauts spent more than eight hours on a space walk, wrestling a four-ton communications satellite, Intelsat-VI, into the cargo bay. There they fitted a new rocket motor and sent the satellite off on its true orbit, 22,300 miles above the Earth.

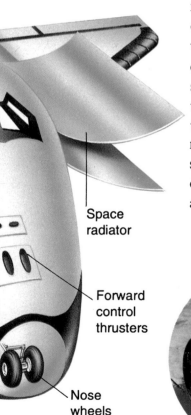

Space radiator

Forward control thrusters

Nose wheels

Disaster

In America's worst space disaster, hot gases leaked through a joint in the booster casing during the launch of Challenger in 1986. A tongue of flame burned into the main tank and ignited the fuel, blowing the shuttle to pieces and killing its seven crew members, among them Christa McAuliffe, a teacher. The disaster set back the program by nearly three years, as engineers struggled to prevent it from ever happening again.

ROCKETS FOR RENT

Today, space has become big business. Rockets can be rented from several suppliers, to launch commercial satellites into orbit. The main players are NASA and the European Space Agency, but Japan, China and what remains of the Soviet space organization are also interested in the market. After a poor start, ESA's Ariane launchers have proved very reliable. The Challenger disaster of 1986 slowed the United States' effort, and opened up the market. By early next century, ESA hopes that Ariane 5 will be able to put a manned European shuttle, Hermes, into space.

Equator launch

The Ariane launch site is at Kourou in French Guyana (right). A rocket launched close to the Equator takes greatest advantage of the Earth's speed of rotation, so needs less thrust than it would if launched from Europe. Surrounded by jungle, the Kourou site has three launch pads, assembly buildings and a control center (below).

Different payloads

A rocket's cargo is its payload. Commercial rockets carry a huge variety of payloads, including satellites for scientific research, communications, navigation, monitoring the weather, and mapping the Earth. Sometimes more than one satellite can be launched on the same mission, sharing costs (right).

Booster integration building

Launch preparation site

Launch pads

Control center

Final assembly building

Military launches

Some 2,000 military satellites have been launched by the United States alone in the past 20 years. Many military launches are kept secret, but usually involve satellites for spying, military communications, or precise navigation. Spy satellites have tended to increase confidence between the superpowers.

Italian space program

In 1988, the Italian government set up the Italian Space Agency, with a budget of more than $1 billion for its first two years. The agency is responsible for Italy's own satellites and for taking part in ESA programs. One of Italy's satellite and communications centers is sited near Palermo, Sicily (above). Its Marcos satellites are designed to study the atmosphere.

International interest

Britain, France, Canada, Germany, India, Brazil, and Japan (inset below) all have special interest in satellites.

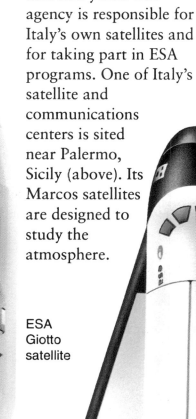

ESA Giotto satellite

Japan's H-1 rocket

Proposed Hermes space orbiter

Microchip technology

The demand for electronic devices on board satellites has been a great stimulus to the development of microchips, now found in a huge range of consumer products, from pocket TVs to laptop computers. These devices have increased the capacity and reliability of weather, communications, military, and spy satellites.

LIVING IN SPACE

While the United States planned Moon missions and shuttles, the former Soviet Union was concentrating on manned space stations and space probes to the planets. Soviet cosmonauts hold all the records for endurance in space. Colonel Yuri Romanenko, the most experienced space traveler of all, has spent more than a year of his life in space, on three separate missions. The most recent was aboard the Mir space station, launched in February 1986. Since its launch Mir has been continually occupied by a series of crews sent up in Soyuz spacecraft, the first permanent manned outpost in space. The cosmonauts spend their time carrying out experiments and making observations of the Earth.

Skylab
The Skylab space station (below and right), made from an empty Saturn IVB rocket tank, was put into orbit in 1973. It was an unlucky craft, requiring a tricky space walk to unfold its solar panels. It finally reentered the atmosphere, breaking up over Australia. It was in orbit for six years but in use for only six months.

Close companions
Living for months in a small space can be difficult. Yuri Grechko and Romanenko (on the left in the circular photo opposite) agreed to share responsibility for routine tasks and mistakes.

A 24-hour day
Although there is no day or night, astronauts keep to a 24-hour routine, which suits the human body best.

A change of staff
Soyuz transfer craft for changing crews dock on one of the docking ports on the end of the Mir station. A fuel tanker is docked at the other end.

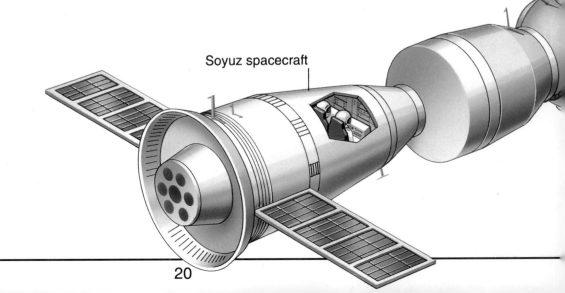

Soyuz spacecraft

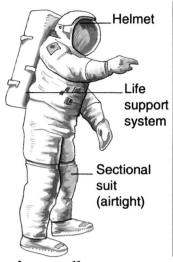

Helmet

Life support system

Sectional suit (airtight)

Keeping fit in space
The bones of early space dwellers became brittle, and their muscles wasted away. They had problems readjusting to gravity on Earth. Today, astronauts counteract these effects through exercise and regular medical checks (right).

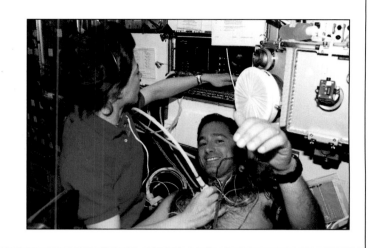

Out for a walk
For space walks astronauts wear a pressurized space suit, usually with a back-pack. It contains supplies of oxygen, as in the case of the Apollo lunar explorers, or small gas jets for moving about, in the Manned Maneuvering Unit (MMU) above.

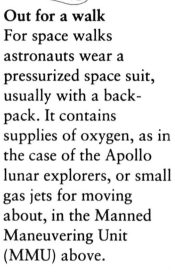

Space sickness
Living in space affects some astronauts quite badly, causing sickness for the first few days. This is due to the brain receiving strange messages from the balance organs inside the ears.

Airlock

Unmanned tanker

◄ Space station Mir
Mir is about 36 feet long and 14 feet in diameter. Most of it is living accommodation for a crew of two. Its large solar panels convert sunlight to electricity.

Working and dining table

Meteorite shield

SATELLITE REVOLUTION

Today, 35 years since Sputnik went into space, there are hundreds of satellites in orbit around the Earth. They relay telephone conversations and TV pictures, take pictures of clouds and weather systems, observe the fine detail of the Earth, and provide precise navigational information for ships and planes. Live TV pictures bounce around the world in a miracle of communication that we now take for granted. The satellite revolution is the single most important result of the conquest of space.

Antenna reflector

Deployment

The space shuttle launches satellites from many countries (the one shown below is Mexico's Morelos satellite). They are lifted from its cargo bay with a jointed manipulator arm 50 feet long. Once the satellite has been released and the shuttle has moved a safe distance away, a small rocket on the satellite is fired to move it into position for orbit. This final stage is called deployment.

Antenna feed

Fixed forward solar panel

Thermal radiator

Control thruster

Propellant tank

Traveling wave tube amplifier

Battery pack

Extendible rear solar panel

Predicting the weather

To provide weather forecasts, satellites take pictures of clouds and even hurricanes (right). They measure temperature, humidity, and wind speeds.

Satellite control

Once in orbit, a satellite's exact position can be adjusted by small control thrusters. These are fired by remote control, using radio signals from ground engineers, if the satellite drifts out of position. The solar panels, dishes, and other antennae are folded up to save room during the launch. They are unfolded through radio signals sent from the ground station.

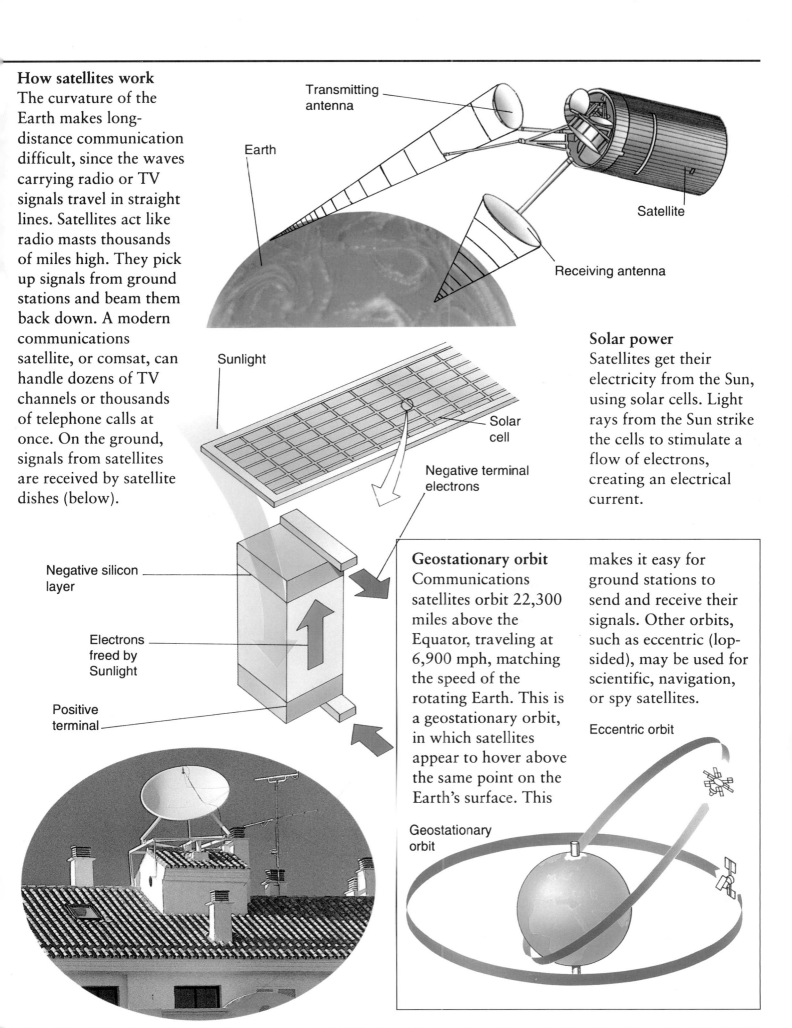

How satellites work

The curvature of the Earth makes long-distance communication difficult, since the waves carrying radio or TV signals travel in straight lines. Satellites act like radio masts thousands of miles high. They pick up signals from ground stations and beam them back down. A modern communications satellite, or comsat, can handle dozens of TV channels or thousands of telephone calls at once. On the ground, signals from satellites are received by satellite dishes (below).

Transmitting antenna

Earth

Satellite

Receiving antenna

Sunlight

Solar cell

Negative terminal electrons

Negative silicon layer

Electrons freed by Sunlight

Positive terminal

Solar power

Satellites get their electricity from the Sun, using solar cells. Light rays from the Sun strike the cells to stimulate a flow of electrons, creating an electrical current.

Geostationary orbit

Communications satellites orbit 22,300 miles above the Equator, traveling at 6,900 mph, matching the speed of the rotating Earth. This is a geostationary orbit, in which satellites appear to hover above the same point on the Earth's surface. This makes it easy for ground stations to send and receive their signals. Other orbits, such as eccentric (lopsided), may be used for scientific, navigation, or spy satellites.

Eccentric orbit

Geostationary orbit

SPIES IN THE SKY

Good generals always try to seize the high ground, and there is nothing higher than a satellite. At least a third of all space launches are military in purpose. Without spy satellites, the intelligence services of the major powers would know very little. Nuclear submarines could not operate without navigation satellites. Secret military communications also depend on satellites. The outcome of recent wars, from the Falklands to the Gulf, has been greatly affected by the use of satellites.

Seeing from space

The clarity of the view from space is remarkable, as is evident from this satellite picture of the fire at the Chernobyl nuclear reactor in 1986. Spy satellites probably cannot read car number plates on Earth, as is often claimed, but they can certainly pick out individual vehicles and even people. Their orbits are often arranged so that they pass over the same spot on the ground when the Sun is in the same position each day, so that changing light and shade do not confuse the images.

Rocket motor

Solar panel

Control thruster

Under cover

When the space shuttle carries military payloads (below), a veil of secrecy is drawn over the mission. The U.S. military even built its own shuttle launch pad at Vandenberg Air Force Base in California, to launch the shuttle on spy missions. It will never be used; the Challenger disaster and other shuttle delays made the military chiefs decide to use ordinary rockets.

Navstar

If nuclear submarines' missiles are to hit their targets, they must know where they are firing from with absolute precision. The U.S. Navstar system was launched in the 1980s. It stands for NAVigation System using Time and Ranging. Each satellite contains three atomic clocks. The system works by measuring the time taken for the signal broadcast by the satellite clocks to reach the user on the ground.

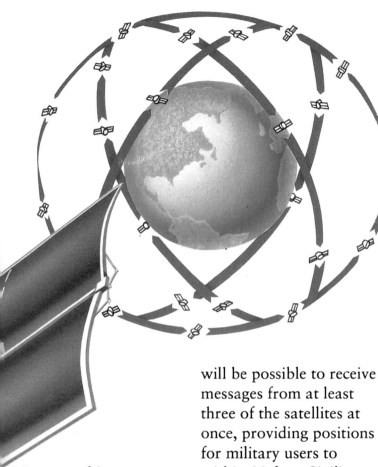

The Gulf War
During the Gulf conflict in 1991, American spy satellites provided vital intelligence about the position and movements of the Iraqi troops occupying Kuwait. Two types of satellite were used: low-orbit ones with telescopes and cameras to take detailed pictures of troop concentrations, airfields (below) and missile launcher sites, and geostationary ones to pick up Iraqi radio, radar, and other signals. Iraq had no such satellites, so was at an enormous disadvantage.

Navstar orbits
Navstar will ultimately have about 20 satellites in three orbits 12,500 miles up. From any point on the Earth, it will be possible to receive messages from at least three of the satellites at once, providing positions for military users to within 30 feet. Civilians can also use Navstar, but not at the same precision; they will know their position to within 300 feet.

SDI
The United States' Strategic Defence Initiative, or "Star Wars," was to be a space-based system for destroying enemy missiles in flight. Announced in 1983, SDI envisaged the use of high-power guns, ground-based rockets, and laser and particle beam weapons. It was an ambitious plan. SDI tests achieved some successes, including shooting down an unmanned aircraft with a laser. The collapse of the Soviet Union in the 1990s means SDI may be scaled down.

Military Salyuts
The Soviet Union launched at least three Salyut space stations devoted to military work. They contained a camera instead of the telescope in the normal Salyut, and the cosmonauts provided information for military exercises as they happened live. Hundreds of unmanned Soviet spy satellites have also been flown.

SECRETS OF THE UNIVERSE

At a fraction of the cost of manned spaceflight, the planetary probes have uncovered far more information in the past 30 years than had been learned in the previous 300. Pioneer 5 was America's first deep space probe, launched in 1960. Mariner 2 was the first probe to visit another planet, Venus, in 1962. Vikings 1 and 2 landed on Mars in 1976. Voyagers 1 and 2 visited the outer planets, taking over ten years to get there. NASA's Hubble space telescope is looking further out into the universe than any Earth-based instrument can.

Antenna

Solar panels

Light shield

Peering into space

Space experts and enthusiasts alike have always been intrigued by the possibility of life elsewhere in the universe. NASA is to use radio telescopes in the biggest-ever search for intelligent extraterrestial life. They will listen to radio signals from stars like our own Sun in the hope of picking up a radio "beacon" from other beings.

▼ The radio telescope at Arecibo, Puerto Rico, has the largest dish in the world.

Scientific instruments command

Origins of the universe

Space research has led some physicists to believe that they are close to understanding how the universe began, with the "Big Bang" theory. Professor Hawking of Cambridge University (below) has researched "black holes," areas of space from which nothing – not even light – can escape.

Space telescope

An Earth telescope looks at space through the atmosphere, which blurs the images it can obtain. The Hubble space telescope was designed to avoid this problem. Its huge mirror collects and reflects faint rays of light from distant stars. An error in grinding the mirror has reduced performance, but a shuttle mission in 1993 should repair the fault.

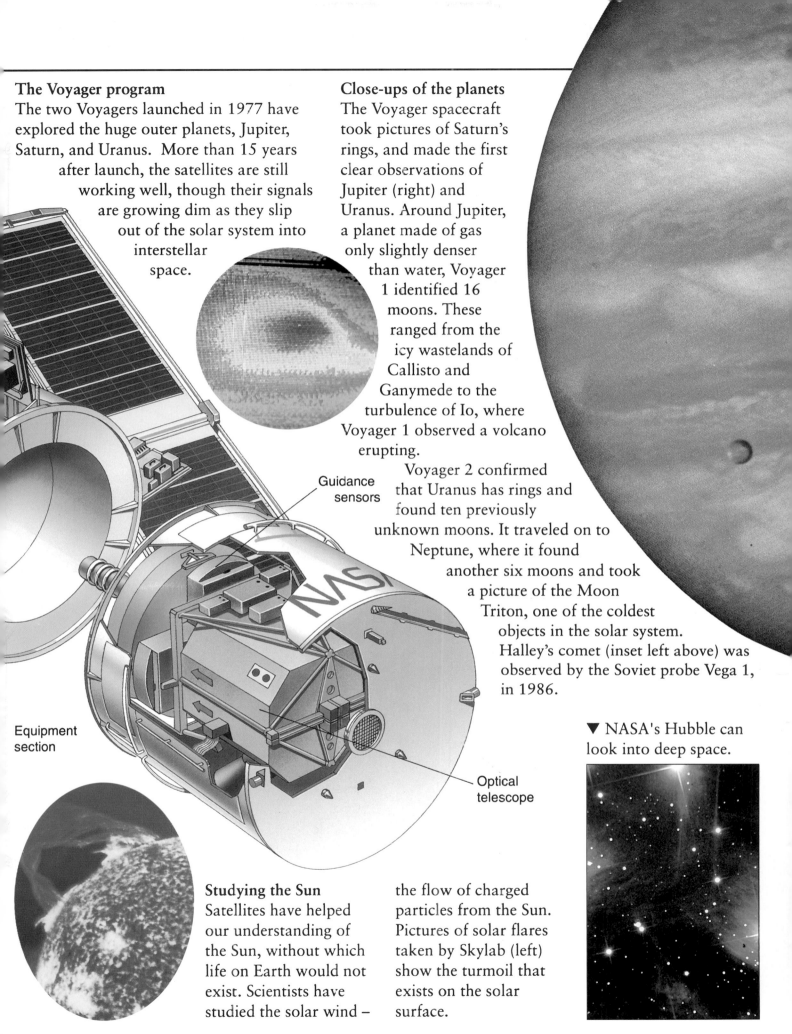

The Voyager program

The two Voyagers launched in 1977 have explored the huge outer planets, Jupiter, Saturn, and Uranus. More than 15 years after launch, the satellites are still working well, though their signals are growing dim as they slip out of the solar system into interstellar space.

Guidance sensors

Equipment section

Close-ups of the planets

The Voyager spacecraft took pictures of Saturn's rings, and made the first clear observations of Jupiter (right) and Uranus. Around Jupiter, a planet made of gas only slightly denser than water, Voyager 1 identified 16 moons. These ranged from the icy wastelands of Callisto and Ganymede to the turbulence of Io, where Voyager 1 observed a volcano erupting.

Voyager 2 confirmed that Uranus has rings and found ten previously unknown moons. It traveled on to Neptune, where it found another six moons and took a picture of the Moon Triton, one of the coldest objects in the solar system. Halley's comet (inset left above) was observed by the Soviet probe Vega 1, in 1986.

Optical telescope

▼ NASA's Hubble can look into deep space.

Studying the Sun

Satellites have helped our understanding of the Sun, without which life on Earth would not exist. Scientists have studied the solar wind – the flow of charged particles from the Sun. Pictures of solar flares taken by Skylab (left) show the turmoil that exists on the solar surface.

THE FUTURE OF SPACE

What next for the space industry? The United States is considering two major projects. One is a permanently manned space station in Earth orbit. The other is a manned trip to Mars. Neither will be easy or cheap. In general, space exploration is very expensive. The Apollo project cost $25 billion; by 1980, the Soviets had spent $45 billion on space missions. With the end of superpower rivalry, space budgets are likely to be cut, since there is less need for rocket missiles or intensive satellite spying. The practical advantages of a permanently manned space station to our everyday lives are doubtful. Manned space flight faces an uncertain future, though unmanned satellites will continue to flourish.

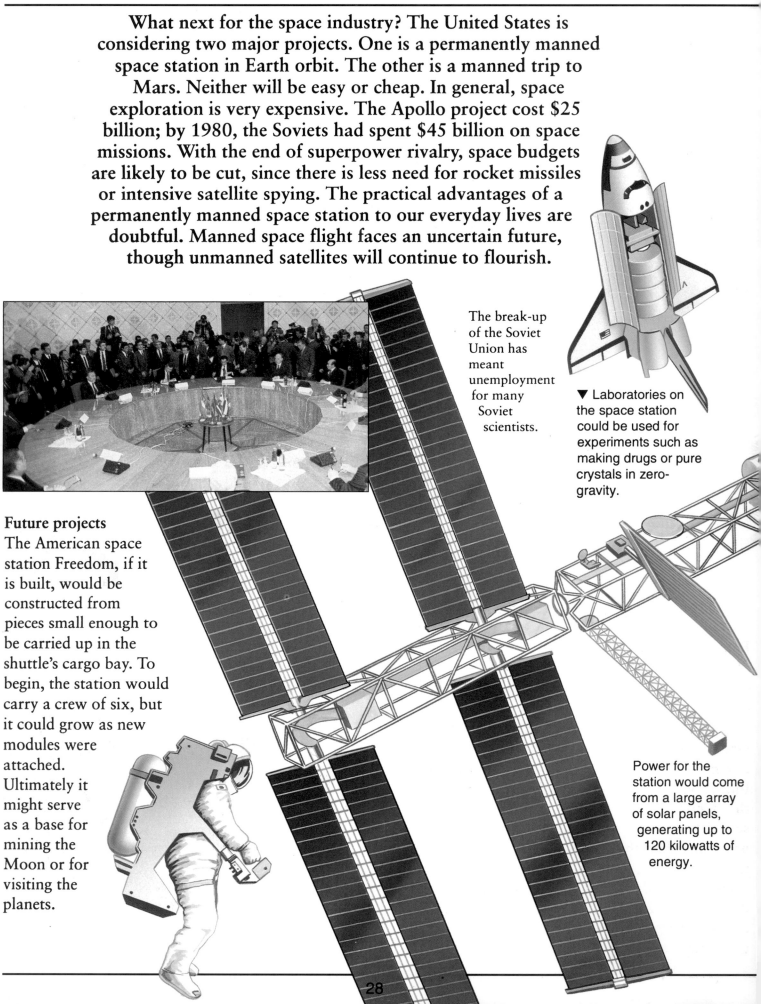

The break-up of the Soviet Union has meant unemployment for many Soviet scientists.

▼ Laboratories on the space station could be used for experiments such as making drugs or pure crystals in zero-gravity.

Future projects
The American space station Freedom, if it is built, would be constructed from pieces small enough to be carried up in the shuttle's cargo bay. To begin, the station would carry a crew of six, but it could grow as new modules were attached. Ultimately it might serve as a base for mining the Moon or for visiting the planets.

Power for the station would come from a large array of solar panels, generating up to 120 kilowatts of energy.

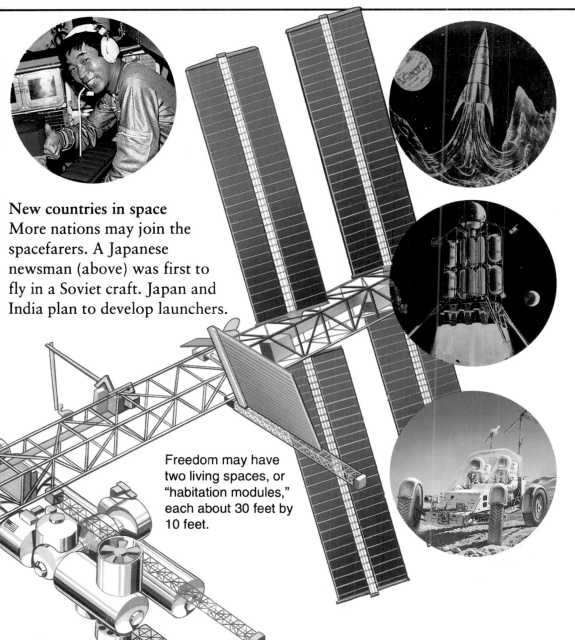

New countries in space
More nations may join the spacefarers. A Japanese newsman (above) was first to fly in a Soviet craft. Japan and India plan to develop launchers.

Freedom may have two living spaces, or "habitation modules," each about 30 feet by 10 feet.

Predictions
Many predictions about space travel have come true: multi-stage rockets and men walking on the Moon, although not quite as conceived in these illustrations from 1927 (top) and 1953 (center). Other predictions have proved false, like the claim by the American astronomer Percival Lowell that there is life on Mars. Today, predictions still flourish. One is that life will be found elsewhere, but it may be billions of miles away. Another is that we may make Mars habitable by changing its climate and creating a breathable atmosphere. More realistically, spaceplanes may carry passengers halfway around the Earth in a few hours, and astronauts may explore and mine the Moon (left).

Employment
Huge numbers of people have been employed in the space and defense industries, which now face a diminished future. In the former Soviet Union, thousands of space scientists are unemployed. In the West the sitution is not so acute, but the days of dramatic, prestige-creating space spectaculars may be over.

Fuels of the future
To reach any planet in a reasonable time, a rocket would need a new form of propulsion. The best prospect is the nuclear rocket, in which heat from a reactor creates a jet of gas to propel the spacecraft. Traveling outside the solar system (right) remains a dream.

CHRONOLOGY

1903 Konstantin Tsiolkovsky publishes his scientific paper on the use of rockets for space travel
1923 German scientist Herman Oberth publishes a book on the technical problems of space flight
1926 Robert Goddard launches the first liquid-propellant rocket
1942 A German A-4 rocket reaches a height of 60 miles. The A-4 is the prototype of the V-2 rocket, developed by Wernher von Braun
1949 An American

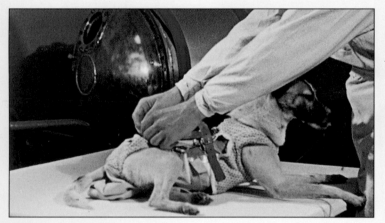
▲ Space dog Laika

rocket, the WAC Corporal, launched as a second stage with a captured German V-2 rocket, reaches a record height of 245 miles
1957 October The Soviet Union launches Sputnik 1, the first artificial satellite
November Launch of Sputnik 2, with dog Laika

1958 January First U.S. satellite, Explorer 1, launched
April Foundation of the United States' National Aeronautics and Space Administration (NASA)
December NASA launches first communications satellite
1959 February First weather satellite, NASA's Vanguard 2
1961 April Soviet Cosmonaut Yuri Gagarin is the first man in space. His Vostok 1 makes a single orbit of the Earth
May Alan Shepard is the

first American in space
August Cosmonaut Gherman Titov orbits the Earth 16 times
1962 February John Glenn is the first American to orbit the Earth
April Ranger 4 is the first probe from the United States to strike the Moon
1963 June Cosmonaut

▲ Mercury crewmen

Valentina Tereshkova is the first woman in space
1964 October Three cosmonauts orbit the Earth in Voskhod 1
1965 March NASA's first manned Gemini flight
July US probe Mariner 4 photographs Mars
1966 January Soviet probe Luna 9 lands on the Moon
1967 January Three Apollo astronauts killed in a launch pad fire
June Soviet probe Venera 4 transmits data on Venus' atmosphere
1968 October First manned Apollo flight
December Three astronauts orbit the Moon in Apollo 8
1969 July Apollo astronauts Neil Armstrong and Edwin Aldrin become the first men on the Moon
1971 May Capsule from Soviet probe Mars 3 lands on Mars
November NASA's probe Mariner 9 is the first to orbit Mars

1973 May Skylab 2 launched with a crew of three
1975 July NASA's Apollo spacecraft docks with a Soyuz craft
October Soviet probe Venera 9 lands on Venus and photographs the planet's surface
1976 July NASA's Viking 1 sends photographs from Mars
1977 August, September NASA launches Voyagers 1 and 2
1979 September U.S. probe Pioneer-Saturn flies past Saturn and

▲ Soviet Lunakhod

transmits photographs and data to Earth
1981 April Launch of Columbia, NASA's first space shuttle, with astronauts John Young and Robert Crippen
1983 June U.S. probe Pioneer 10 becomes the first spacecraft to travel beyond all the planets
November Spacelab, built by the European Space Agency (ESA) is

▲ Romanenko (left)

first launched by space shuttle

1986 January Space shuttle Challenger

▲ Manned Maneuvreing Unit

explodes shortly after launch, killing its crew of seven. U.S. manned space program grounded, pending investigation of the Challenger disaster
February Launch of

Soviet space station Mir
March ESA's probe Giotto passes Halley's comet and sends data and photographs
1987 May Soviet rocket Energia first launched
1988 September U.S. manned space program resumed with launch of shuttle Discovery
November Unmanned Soviet space shuttle Buran launched by Energia
1990 Hubble Space Telescope launched
1992 May U.S. space shuttle astronauts repair Intelsat-VI in space.
Cosmic Background Explorer satellite discovers the oldest light in the universe

Astronaut
The word for a space pilot used by the West and the United States

Booster
A rocket engine strapped to a spacecraft to give it extra thrust during the first seconds after launch. It is usually jettisoned after use

Cosmonaut
The term for a space pilot used by the Soviet Union

Geostationary orbit
A common flight path of satellites above the Earth's equator. A satellite in geostationary orbit keeps pace with the rotation of the Earth, appearing to hover over the same spot on the Earth's surface

Launcher
A launch vehicle, or rocket engine, that carries a payload into space

Module
A section of a spacecraft that can be separated from other sections

Orbit
The flight path of a spacecraft or satellite circling the Earth, Moon, or a planet

Payload
A rocket's cargo, such as a satellite

Probe
An unmanned spacecraft

Propellant
The substance burned in a rocket engine to produce thrust

Oxidizer
Substance containing oxygen that mixes with the fuel in a rocket engine and enables the fuel to burn

Satellite
An object orbiting a larger one. The Moon is a natural satellite of the Earth. There are now many artificial or man-made satellites orbiting the Earth

Stage
One section of a rocket

Thrust
The pushing force generated by a rocket's engine

Thruster
Small rocket used to make minor adjustments to a spacecraft's position

INDEX

Aldrin, Buzz 13
anti-missle satellites 4, 25
Apollo spacecraft 12, 13, 28
Ariane rocket 14, 18
Armstrong, Neil 13
astonauts 11, 20, 21, 31
Atlas rocket 14

Bell rocket plane 16
Big Bang theory 26
black holes 26
booster rockets 5, 14, 31
Buran space shuttle 5

Challenger space shuttle 15, 17
Cold War 4, 8
Collins, Michael 13
Columbia space shuttle 17
communications satellites 4, 9, 17, 23
cosmonauts 10, 20, 31
costs of space exploration 16, 28

Early Bird satellite 9
eccentric orbit 23
Energia rocket 5, 14
European Space Agency (ESA) 14, 18, 19
Explorer 1 satellite 9

Freedom space station 28, 29
fuels 15, 29

Gagarin, Yuri 10
Gemini spacecraft 10
geostationary orbit 23, 31
Glenn, John 10,11
Goddard, Robert 6

gravity 5, 14, 21
Grechko, Yuri 20
Gulf War 25

Halley's comet 27
Hawking, Stephen 26
Hermes space shuttle 18
Hitler, Adolf 7
Hubble space telescope 26, 27
hydrogen 15

India 19, 29
Intelsat-VI satellite 17
Italian Space Agency 19

Japan 14, 18, 19, 29
Jupiter 27
Jupiter C rocket 9

Kennedy, John F. 11
Korolyev, Sergei 8
Kourou 18

Laika 9
launchers 8, 11, 14, 29, 31
Leonov, Alexsei 11
living in space 20, 21

Manned Maneuvering Unit (MMU) 21
manned space flight 10, 11, 14, 28
Marcos satellite 19
Mariner space probe 26
Mars 26, 28, 29
Mercury spacecraft 9, 10
microchip technology 19
military satellites 19, 24-25
Mir space station 20, 21

modules 29, 31
Moon landings 11, 12-13, 29
Morelos satellite 22
multi-stage rockets 5, 14, 29

NASA 9, 12, 13, 18, 26
navigation satellites 24-25
Navstar system 24-25
Neptune 27
nuclear-powered rockets 29

orbits 23, 24, 31
origins of the universe 26
oxidizers 15, 31

payloads 14, 18, 24, 31
Pioneer space probe 26
planetary exploration 26, 27
propellants 6, 7, 15, 29, 31

Redstone rocket 14
rockets 6-7, 8, 12, 14-15, 16, 18, 29
Romanenko, Yuri 20

Salyut space station 25
satellite dishes 23
satellites 4, 8, 9, 14, 17, 18-19, 22-25, 27, 28, 31
Saturn 27
Saturn V rocket 12
Skylab space station 20, 27
solar power 21, 23, 28
solar wind 27
Soviet Union 8, 10, 11, 13, 14, 20, 25, 28, 29
Soyuz spacecraft 13, 20
space industry 5, 29

space probes 26, 27, 31
space race 11
space shuttles 5, 16-17, 22, 24
space sickness 21
space stations 20, 21, 25, 28
space suits 21
space technology 4, 5, 8, 15, 19, 28
space telescopes 26, 27
space walks 11, 17, 20, 21
spaceplanes 29
Sputnik satellite 8, 9
spy satellites 19, 24, 25
SS-6 rocket 8
stages 14, 31
Star Wars 25
Strategic Defense Initiative (SDI) 25
Sun 27
Surveyor spacecraft 13

Telstar satellite 9
thrust 6, 7, 31
thrusters 22, 31
Triton 27
Tsiolkovsky, Konstantin 6

United States 8, 9, 10, 11, 13, 14, 19, 24, 25, 28
Uranus 27

V-2 rocket 7
van Allen belts 9
Vanguard rocket 9
Verne, Jules 7
VFR rocket 6
von Braun, Wernher 7, 9, 12
Voshkod spacecraft 11
Vostok spacecraft 10, 11
Voyager space probe 26, 27